FRANÉ LESSAC

CARIBBEAN ALPHABET

TAMBOURINE BOOKS · NEW YORK

Copyright © 1989 by Frané Lessac

First published in Great Britain by the Macmillan Press Ltd

All rights reserved. No part of this book may be reproduced or utilized in any form or by any means, electronic or

mechanical, including photocopying, recording, or by any information storage or retrieval system, without permission in writing

from the Publisher. Inquiries should be addressed toTambourine Books, a division of William Morrow & Company, Inc.,

1350 Avenue of the Americas, New York, New York 10019. The illustrations were painted in gouache on paper.

The text type is Helvetica Rounded. Printed in the United States of America.

Library of Congress Cataloging in Publication Data

Lessac, Frané. Caribbean alphabet/Frané Lessac. — 1st U.S. ed. p. cm. Summary: Presents an alphabet of

images from the Caribbean, such as hibiscus, mangoes, and reggae. 1. Caribbean, English-speaking — Description and

travel — Dictionaries, Juvenile. 2. Caribbean, English-speaking — Dictionaries, Juvenile. [1. Caribbean Area. 2. Alphabet.]

I. Title. F2130.L47 1994 421'.1[E] — dc20 93-15833 CIP AC ISBN 0-688-12952-8. — ISBN 0-688-12953-6 (lib. bdg.)

First U.S. edition, 1994

1 3 5 7 9 10 8 6 4 2

For Arthur and Rosemary

airport arrivals airplane agouti

B boat birds breadfruit bananas

cricket coconut cat cows

donkeys dolphins dasheen

egrets eggs estuary eels

fort fisherman frogs flowers

goats grass gate gazebo

house   hummingbirds   hibiscus

island   iguanas   inlet

jump-up Junkanoo

kids kites kittens knots

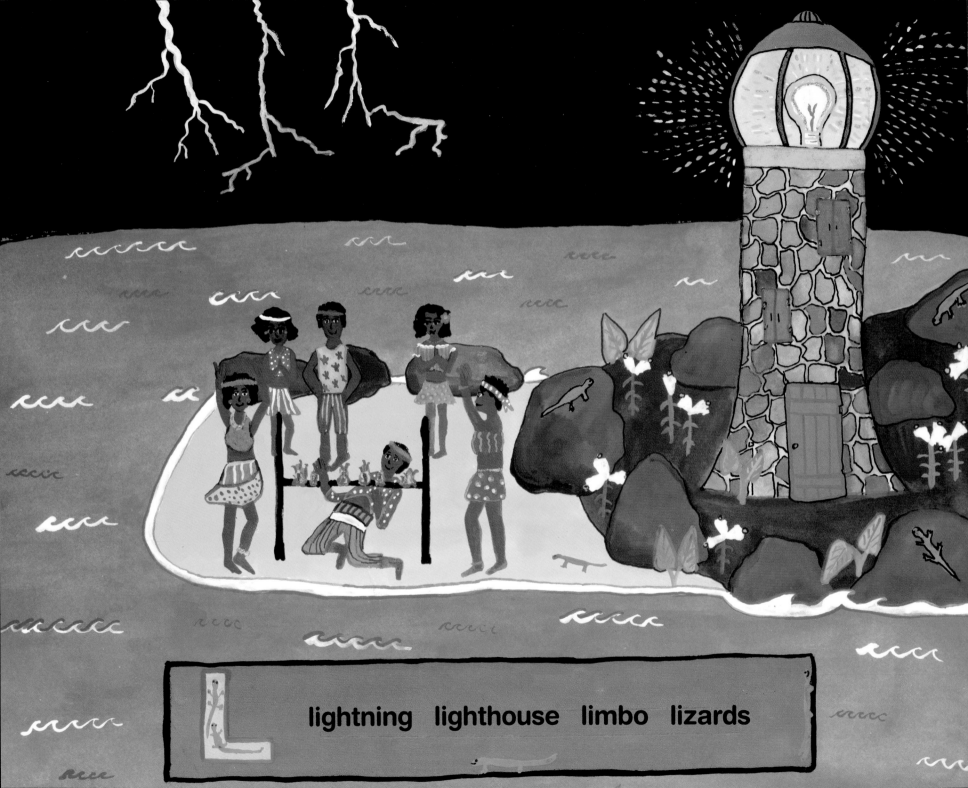

lightning lighthouse limbo lizards

mountains   market   mangoes   melons

nutmeg nets nuts nests

ocean   orange   oars   octopus

pirate pelican pineapples pawpaws

quay queen-conch

rainbow Rastafarians reggae radio

steelband   sand   starfish   seashells

tourists towels turtles treasure

university   uniforms   umbrellas

village view volcano valley

whale wharf watermelons waves

x marks the spot

Yin-Yang

Y18

yellow yacht

 zoo zebra zookeeper zzzz

GLOSSARY

Agouti
A furry, rabbit-sized rodent of the West Indies.

Breadfruit
A tropical fruit that, when baked, tastes like bread.

Dasheen
The taro plant, whose root is a popular Caribbean vegetable.

Egret
A bird of the heron family.

Hibiscus
A colorful flowering plant.

Iguana
A tropical lizard.

Junkanoo
A Caribbean festival celebrated over the Christmas holidays on various islands, often featuring the folk dance known as Jump-up.

Pawpaw
The sweet fruit of the papaya tree.

Queen-conch
A sea snail prized for its shell.

Rastafarians
Followers of a Jamaican cultural and religious movement.

Reggae
An internationally popular Jamaican style of music.

Steelband
Musicians playing instruments first fashioned in Trinidad out of old barrels and oil drums.